PIANO · VOCAL · GUI

CMT 40G DRINKING SONGS

ISBN-13: 978-1-4234-2501-4
ISBN-10: 1-4234-2501-4

HAL·LEONARD®
CORPORATION

7777 W. BLUEMOUND RD. P.O. BOX 13819 MILWAUKEE, WI 53213

Visit Hal Leonard Online at
www.halleonard.com

CMT 40 GREATEST DRINKING SONGS

RANK	SONG	ARTIST
1	Friends in Low Places	Garth Brooks
2	Family Tradition	Hank Williams, Jr.
3	Don't Come Home a Drinkin' (With Lovin' on Your Mind)	Loretta Lynn
4	Whiskey River	Willie Nelson
5	Sunday Mornin' Comin' Down	Johnny Cash
6	All My Rowdy Friends Are Coming over Tonight	Hank Williams, Jr.
7	I Think I'll Just Stay Here and Drink	Merle Haggard
8	White Lightning	George Jones
9	Chug-A-Lug	Roger Miller
10	You Ain't Much Fun	Toby Keith
11	There Stands the Glass	Webb Pierce
12	Longneck Bottle	Garth Brooks with Steve Wariner
13	There's a Tear in My Beer	Various Artists
14	Straight Tequila Night	John Anderson
15	Pop a Top	Alan Jackson
16	Whiskey Bent and Hell Bound	Hank Williams, Jr.
17	I'm Gonna Hire a Wino to Decorate Our Home	David Frizzell
18	It's Five O'Clock Somewhere	Alan Jackson & Jimmy Buffett
19	Drinkin' My Baby Goodbye	Charlie Daniels
20	The Whiskey Ain't Workin'	Travis Tritt & Marty Stuart
21	Two More Bottles of Wine	Various Artists
22	Set 'Em Up Joe	Vern Gosdin
23	You Never Even Call Me by My Name	David Allan Coe
24	Don't the Girls All Get Prettier at Closin' Time	Mickey Gilley
25	The Bottle Let Me Down	Merle Haggard
26	Whiskey, If You Were a Woman	Highway 101
27	Wine into Water	T. Graham Brown
28	What's Made Milwaukee Famous (Has Made a Loser Out of Me)	Jerry Lee Lewis
29	Two Piña Coladas	Garth Brooks
30	Beer for My Horses	Toby Keith & Willie Nelson
31	Ten Rounds with Jose Cuervo	Tracy Byrd
32	Tequila Sunrise	Eagles
33	Wasted Days and Wasted Nights	Freddy Fender
34	Tonight the Heartache's on Me	Dixie Chicks
35	Beer Thirty	Brooks & Dunn
36	Naked Women and Beer	Hank Williams, Jr.
37	That's Why I'm Here	Kenny Chesney
38	I Love This Bar	Toby Keith
39	Killin' Time	Clint Black
40	Beer Run (B Double E Double Are You In?)	George Jones with Garth Brooks

CONTENTS

Alphabetical by Song

ALL MY ROWDY FRIENDS ARE COMING OVER TONIGHT

Words and Music by
HANK WILLIAMS, JR.

got to get read - y, make ev - 'ry-thing right, 'cause all my row - dy friends are com - in'

o - ver to - night. _____ Do you wan - na

drink? Hey, do you wan - na par - ty? _____

Hey, hon - ey this is ole Hank, _____ { read - y to get the thing } { read - y to get the music }

Hey, do you wan - na par - ty? ___ Hey, this is rock - in'

Ran - dall Hank, ___ come on and get your mo - tor start - ed. I cooked a

pig in the ground, got some beer on ice, ___ and all my row-dy friends are com-in' o - ver to - night. ___

Additional Lyrics

2. But I've got some natural queens out on the floor,
   And ole Miss Mississippi just walked through the door.
   Got a little whirlpool just made for ten,
   And you can jump out, you can jump in.
   You can do anything that you want to do,
   But uh-uh don't you step on my cowboy boots.

BEER FOR MY HORSES

Words and Music by TOBY KEITH
and SCOTT EMERICK

meet back at the lo-cal sa-loon. ___ We'll raise up our glass - es a - gainst ___

___ e - vil forc - es, sing - ing, "Whis-key for my men, _____ beer for my hors -

To Coda ⊕

- es."

We got too ___ man - y gang - sters do - ing dirt - y deeds. _ We've got

BEER RUN
(B Double E Double Are You In?)

Words and Music by KIM WILLIAMS, GEORGE DUCAS,
AMANDA WILLIAMS, KEITH ANDERSON and KENT BLAZY

BEER THIRTY

Words and Music by RONNIE DUNN
and TERRY McBRIDE

I got a six pack, got a
I put in my for - ty,

It's beer thir - ty, a honk - y tonk time. _____

time. _____

THE BOTTLE LET ME DOWN

Words and Music by
MERLE HAGGARD

night your mem - 'ry found me much too so - ber.
wine don't take ef - fect me the way it used to.

To Coda ⊕

Could - n't drink e - nough to keep you off my
I'm hurt - in' in an old fa - mil - iar

D

mind. To - night the bot - tle let me

down, and let your

CHUG-A-LUG

Words and Music by
ROGER MILLER

DON'T COME HOME A DRINKIN'
(With Lovin' on Your Mind)

Words and Music by LORETTA LYNN
and PEGGY SUE WELLS

Well, you thought I'd be wait-in' up ___ when
nev-er take me an-y-where ___ be-

you came home last night.
cause you're al-ways gone. You'd been out with all the boys ___ and you
And man-y a night ___ I've laid a-wake ___ and

DON'T THE GIRLS ALL GET PRETTIER AT CLOSIN' TIME

Words and Music by
BAKER KNIGHT

DRINKIN' MY BABY GOODBYE

Words and Music by
CHARLIE DANIELS

Sit - tin' on a bar-stool act - in' like a durn fool, that's what I'm a-do-in' to-day. Sit - tin' here drink - in', try'n' to keep from think - in', I'm a-booz-in' my trou-bles a - way. Well, now

FAMILY TRADITION

Words and Music by
HANK WILLIAMS, JR.

1. Coun-try mu-sic sing-ers have al-ways been a real close fam-i-
2.,3. (See additional lyrics)

ly, but late-ly some of my kin-folk have dis-

owned a few oth-ers and me. I guess it's be-

car - ry - in' on ___ an old fam - 'ly tra - di - tion. ___

di - tion. ___

Additional Lyrics

2. I am very proud of my daddy's name,
   Although his kind of music and mine ain't exactly the same.
   Stop and think it over, put yourself in my position.
   If I get stoned and sing all night long, it's a family tradition.

   So don't ask me, "Hank,
   Why do you drink?
   Hank, why do you roll smoke?
   Why must you live out the songs that you wrote?"
   If I'm down in a honky tonk, some old slicks tryin' to give me friction
   I say leave me alone, I'm singin' all night long, it's a family tradition.

3. Lordy, I have loved some ladies and I have loved Jim Beam,
   And they both tried to kill me in Nineteen Seventy-Three.
   When that doctor asked me, "Son, how'd you get in this condition?"
   I said, "Hey sawbones, I'm just carryin' on an old family tradition."

   So don't ask me, "Hank,
   Why do you drink?
   Hank, why do you roll smoke?
   Why must you live out the songs that you wrote?"
   Stop and think it over, try to put yourself in my unique position.
   If I get stoned and sing all night long, it's a family tradition.

FRIENDS IN LOW PLACES

Words and Music by DeWAYNE BLACKWELL
and EARL BUD LEE

Well, I

I've got friends __ in low plac - es where the

whis - key _____ drowns _____ and the beer _____ chas - es my blues _____

I LOVE THIS BAR

Words and Music by TOBY KEITH
and SCOTT EMERICK

I THINK I'LL JUST STAY HERE AND DRINK

Words and Music by
MERLE HAGGARD

I'M GONNA HIRE A WINO TO DECORATE OUR HOME

Words and Music by
DEWAYNE BLACKWELL

LONGNECK BOTTLE

Words and Music by RICK CARNES
and STEVE WARINER

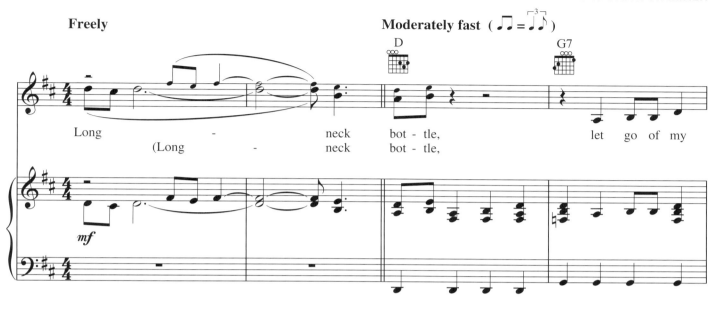

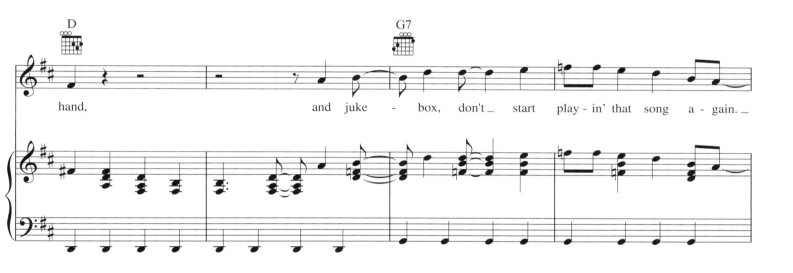

IT'S FIVE O'CLOCK SOMEWHERE

Words and Music by JIM BROWN
and DON ROLLINS

It's five ___ o'-clock some - where.

Repeat and Fade

ad lib.

Optional Ending

KILLIN' TIME

Words and Music by CLINT BLACK
and HAYDEN NICHOLAS

NAKED WOMEN AND BEER

Words and Music by
HANK WILLIAMS, JR.

and down and all _____ a - round _ the stage. _

But when the wom - en start tak - in' their clothes _ off, now

we have got some strange _ laws, the most hyp - o - crit - i - cal thing _

_ a - round _ these days. _ 'Cause where

POP A TOP

Words and Music by
NAT STUCKEY

To Coda

SET 'EM UP JOE

Words and Music by HANK COCHRAN,
BUDDY CANNON, VERN GOSDIN
and DEAN DILLON

STRAIGHT TEQUILA NIGHT

Words and Music by DEBBIE HUPP
and KENT ROBBINS

Don't ask ___ her on a straight te - qui - la night. ___ She'll start think - ing a - bout ___ him, then she's read - y to fight. Blames her bro - ken heart ___ ___ on ev - 'ry man in sight ___ on a straight te - qui - la night.

Repeat and Fade

SUNDAY MORNIN' COMIN' DOWN

Words and Music by
KRIS KRISTOFFERSON

TEN ROUNDS WITH JOSE CUERVO

Words and Music by CASEY BEATHARD,
MICHAEL P. HEENEY and MARLA CANNON-GOODMAN

When I walked in, ___ the band ___ just start-ed. The sing-er could-n't car-ry a tune ___ in a buck-et. Was on a

Then some stran-ger asked ___ me to dance and I re-vealed ___ to her ___ my ___ two ___ left ___ feet. Said, "Don't

Well, a-round five ___ or round six, ___ I for-got ___ what I came ___

TEQUILA SUNRISE

Words and Music by DON HENLEY
and GLENN FREY

It's an-oth-er te-qui - la sun - rise

star - in' slow - ly 'cross ___ the sky, ___

THAT'S WHY I'M HERE

Words and Music by SHAYE SMITH
and MARK ALAN SPRINGER

THERE STANDS THE GLASS

Words by RUSS HULL,
MARY JEAN SHURTZ and AUDREY GREISHAM
Music by RUSS HULL

THERE'S A TEAR IN MY BEER

Words and Music by
HANK WILLIAMS

A7 / D

tears will leave my eyes. }
heart won't hurt me so. }

There's a tear in my

beer 'cause I'm cry-in' for you, dear.

E7 / A7 / **1** D Fdim

You are on my lone-ly mind. _____

A7 / **2** D Em Em/A D

_____ Last _____ mind. _____

WASTED DAYS AND WASTED NIGHTS

Words and Music by WAYNE M. DUNCAN
and FREDDY FENDER

TONIGHT THE HEARTACHE'S ON ME

Words and Music by MARY FRANCIS,
JOHN MacRAE and BOB MORRISON

TWO MORE BOTTLES OF WINE

Words and Music by
DELBERT McCLINTON

Moderate Country Rock

We came out __ west to-geth __ er with a com-mon de-sire. __
way he left sure __ turned __ my __ head a-round. __

The fe-ver we had __ might-a
Seemed like o-ver-night he just

set the west coast on __ fire.
up and put me down. __

Two months
Well, __ ain't gon-na

TWO PIÑA COLADAS

Words and Music by SANDY MASON,
BENITA MARIE HILL and SHAWN CAMP

Moderately bright

I was feel-in' the blues, __ I was watch-ing the news, __ when this
I've got-ta say __ that the wind and the waves __ and the

fel-la came on __ T.V. He said, "I'm tell-in' you __ that
moon wink-in' down __ at me eas-es my mind __ by

sci-ence has prov-en that heart-aches are healed by __ the sea. __
leav-in' be-hind __ the heart-aches that love __ of-ten brings. __ Now

WHAT'S MADE MILWAUKEE FAMOUS
(Has Made a Loser Out of Me)

Words and Music by
GLENN SUTTON

WHISKEY RIVER

Words and Music by
J.B. SHIN III

Whis - key Riv - er, take my mind. Don't let her

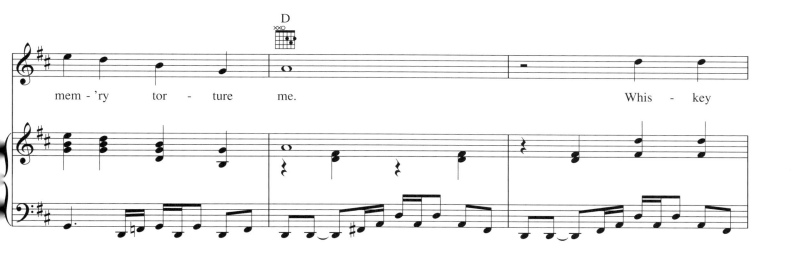

mem - 'ry tor - ture me. Whis - key

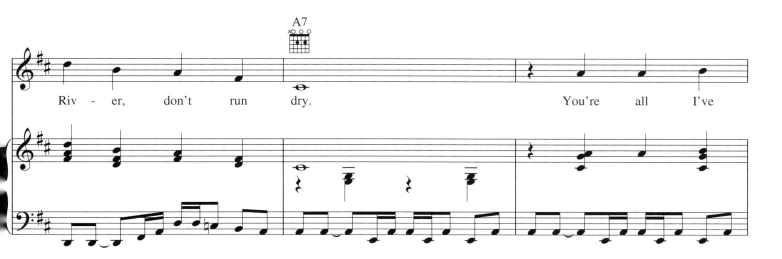

Riv - er, don't run dry. You're all I've

THE WHISKEY AIN'T WORKIN'

Words and Music by RONNY SCAIFE
and MARTY STUART

WHISKEY BENT AND HELL BOUND

Words and Music by
HANK WILLIAMS, JR.

Sure e-nough a-bout

You know Hank's __

__ songs al-ways make me feel low down.

WHISKEY, IF YOU WERE A WOMAN

By MARY WELCH,
JOHNNY MacRAE AND BOB MORRISON

WHITE LIGHTNING

Words and Music by
J.P. RICHARDSON

WINE INTO WATER

Words and Music by T. GRAHAM BROWN,
BRUCE BURCH and TED HEWITT

once up-on ___ a time ___ You turned the wa - ter in - to wine. ___

___ And now on my knees I'm turn-ing to You, Fa -

- ther. Could You help me turn ___ the wine ___ back in - to wa -

To Coda ⊕

1

- ter?

YOU NEVER EVEN CALL ME BY MY NAME

Words and Music by
STEVE GOODMAN

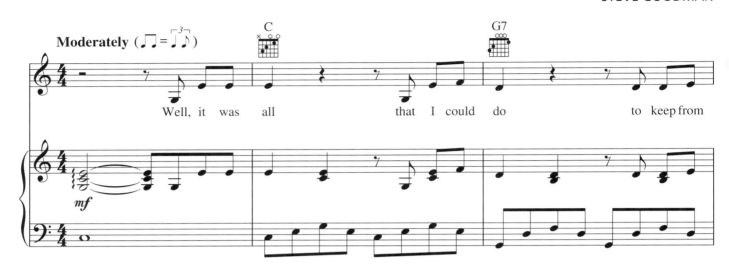

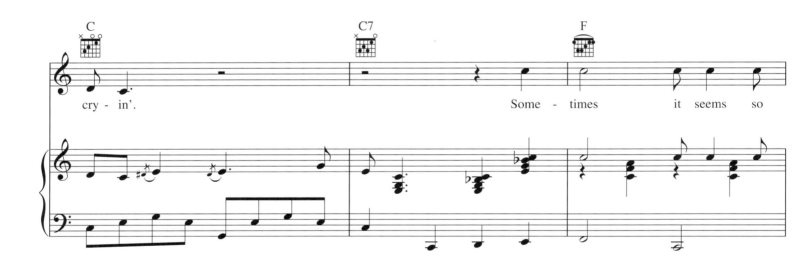

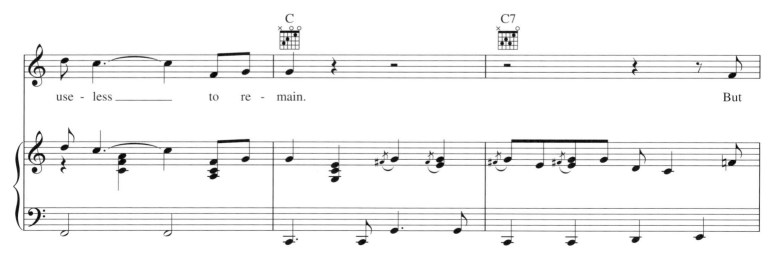

YOU AIN'T MUCH FUN

Words and Music by TOBY KEITH
and CARL GOFF, JR.

Moderately

I used to come home late __ and not a min-ute too soon, __ bark-in' like a dog, howl-in' at the moon. You'd be mad __ as an